Decoding the Interview Challenge

Proven Tactics for Job Search Triumph

Yvonne D. Spina

Decoding the Interview Challenge

Copyright

Disclaimer

The data given in this book is for general enlightening purposes as it were. While we endeavor to give precise and exceptional data, we make no portrayals or guarantees of any sort, expressed or suggested, about the culmination, exactness, unwavering quality, appropriateness, or accessibility concerning the data, items, benefits, or related designs held inside the book for any reason. Any reliance you put on such information is severely regardless of bountiful counsel in actuality.

In no occasion will we be at risk for any misfortune or harm, including without impediment, aberrant or important misfortune or harm, or any misfortune or harm at all emerging from loss of information or benefits emerging out of, or regarding, the utilization of this book.

Through books you might have the option to connect to different sites that are not influenced quite a bit by. We have zero influence over the nature, content, and accessibility of those locales. The joining of any associations doesn't ensure to gather an idea or embrace the viewpoints imparted inside them.

Each work is made to keep the book ready without a hitch. In any case, we get a sense of ownership with, and won't be at risk for, books being briefly inaccessible because of specialized issues unchangeable as far as we might be concerned.

Decoding the Interview Challenge

About the author

Meet Yvonne D. Spina, Your Manual for Vocation Change Yvonne D. Spina is something other than a name; she's an energetic supporter for vocation development and a carefully prepared master in the specialty of occupation guiding. With an abundance of involvement and a pledge to direct people toward proficient achievement, Yvonne brings an interesting mix of sympathy and skill to the universe of vocation improvement.

Equipped with a degree in Directing Brain research, Yvonne mixes scholarly information with viable experiences in her way to deal with work guiding. Her obligation to keeping up to date with industry patterns is obvious in her ceaseless support in proficient advancement exercises, guaranteeing that her recommendation isn't just educated yet in addition lined up with the powerful idea of the gig market.

Yvonne's devotion to aiding a more extensive crowd is clear in her job as a creator. Through her composition, she shares bits of knowledge, techniques, and commonsense tips that go past the conventional limits of one-on-one guiding. She wants to demystify the pursuit of the employment process and engage users with the information they need to assume command over their vocation processes.

Yvonne accepts that professional achievement isn't just about getting a new line of work; it's tied in with building a satisfying and Yvonne effectively encourages a strong local area for those exploring the powerful scene of professional improvement. Yvonne is here to enlighten the way ahead.

TABLE OF CONTENT

Decoding the Interview Challenge

INTRODUCTION

A new employee screening is more than basically a gathering in the speedy, serious universe of the present proficient scene; a significant occasion has the ability to decide the course of your profession. Presenting "Decoding the Interview Challenge: Proven Tactics for Job Search Triumph," an inestimable instrument painstakingly intended to assist you with exploring the intricacies of the cutting edge quest for new employment.

Translating the screening is an expertise that makes the aggressive hang out in reality as we know it where chances proliferate however the contest is extreme. This book is something other than an aide; it's an unlimited toolset intended to help ongoing alumni entering the labor force as well as old pros searching for new difficulties.

Set off on an experience that rises above traditional meeting direction. " Deciphering the Meeting Code" investigates the unpretentious subtleties of the recruiting system in a thorough way. Every one of the parts lead to progress in the meeting, from fostering areas of strength for a brand that works in the computerized age to excelling at self-advancement.

We'll go past the overall direction offered somewhere else here. This handbook will be your dependable friend as you explore the complicated landscape of prospective employee meetings. Understanding the brain research fundamental inquiries is similarly just about as significant as giving responses. Expect an exhaustive investigation of exploration methods that go past the organization site as we travel through these sections, alongside counsel on the most proficient method to expert conduct and specialized interviews.

As we dig further into "Decoding the Interview Challenge," prepare to reveal the secrets of the contemporary work scene. This is more than just a manual; it's a strategic accomplice to assist you with cleaning your techniques, work on your capacities, and set yourself in the most ideal situation to prevail in your pursuit of employment. This is where your way to professional achievement starts.

Overview of the importance of mastering interviews in the job search process

Why are meets so significant for landing the position of your fantasies? This is the manner by which it works: interviews are serious business. These are your opportunity to exhibit who you are beyond your resume, they're not only a checkbox in the recruiting system.

Think of it as a discourse that stretches out past your resume; it offers potential bosses a chance to study your character, abilities, and fit into their group. It's your opportunity, at the end of the day, to show that you're more than just an assortment of accomplishments and that you bring something uniquely great to the table for the world.

Prevailing in interviews is a higher priority than simply getting some work; it's tied in with handling the best situation for you. It's tied in with finding a position where you fit in with the organization's way of life as well as satisfying the guidelines. Besides, the work market is dynamic, can we just be real for a minute. What was fruitful yesterday may not be so tomorrow. Along these lines, there is no one-size-fits-all way to deal with meetings. Being adaptable is vital to addressing both normal requests and unanticipated hardships that might emerge.

Consequently, the objective of "Decoding the Interview Challenge" is to assist you with finding the work that impeccably suits your requirements as opposed to only any old work. We'll analyze how to achieve it in the forthcoming parts. We'll go into the particulars of interview achievement, from fostering your own image to dealing with testing conduct requests. Since securing the position you're excited about is a higher priority than simply making a halfhearted effort. Presently how about we set off this way to outcome in the meeting!

The changing landscape of job interviews in today's competitive market

Not exclusively are the undeniable trends moving throughout the prospective employee meeting scene, they are adjusting the fundamental groundworks of our expert connection procedure. Interviews are currently virtual gatherings that occur practically and don't have to happen in that frame of mind of the development of remote work and worldwide availability. Thus, up-and-comers presently need to figure out how to show themselves through screens and become proficient at projecting amazing skill and energy without actual presence.

Moreover, another member has entered the talking field with the presentation of computerized reasoning (man-made intelligence). Man-made intelligence driven appraisals and computerized screening techniques are becoming the norm, which confounds the pursuit of the employment process. As well as talking with recruiting administrators, competitors likewise speak with calculations that sift through resumes and assess reactions to estimate achievement.

Interviews are turning out to be more engaged than just the specialized regions. Surveying an up-and-comer's delicate abilities, social fit, and limit with regards to joint effort in comprehensive and different work environments is turning out to be increasingly more essential to managers. It's not just about what you know; it's likewise about how well you can utilize it to further develop group elements and encourage a solid workplace.

In "Decoding the Interview Challenge," we'll take a gander at the cutting edge capacities expected to prevail in this high speed setting notwithstanding the imperishable meeting achievement ideas. We're here to ensure you're ready to deal with the moving scene of new employee screenings, from dominating video meetings to appreciating and tolerating computer based intelligence helped recruiting systems. Get ready to ride the rushes of development and change as we traverse the changing meeting scene in the present very cutthroat market.

CHAPTER 1:
Understanding the Interview Process

One significant stage in the pursuit of the employment process is the meeting strategy. This presents an opportunity for the two up-and-comers and bosses to acquire extra understanding about one another, the association, and the job. Potential candidates can work on their odds of coming out on top by monitoring the different strides in the screening and knowing what to expect.

Initial interview

A screening interview is much of the time the underlying move toward the screening. This typically comprises a fast telephone discussion or video gathering with an employing supervisor or spotter. Surveying a competitor's reasonableness for the position and essential capabilities is the point of the screening interview. Candidates must be prepared to answer requests with respect to their experience, capabilities, and explanations behind looking for the gig.

First Interview

A candidate will be welcome to an underlying meeting in the event that they endure the screening system. Typically, the enlisting supervisor or a board of questionnaires will direct an in-person interview for this. Contrasted with the screening interview, the underlying meeting is longer and more thorough, covering a bigger scope of subjects like the up-and-comer's experience, capacities, knowledge of the business and the position, and social fit.

Afterwards Interviews

A candidate might be contacted for follow-up interviews if they do well in the first one. For more senior roles or jobs requiring certain expertise or abilities, this is typical. Meetings with various team members, such as the department head, CEO, or other stakeholders, may follow subsequent interviews.

Offer of Employment

The business will extend a job offer if they are pleased with the candidate's performance during the interview process. It is recommended that the candidate thoroughly evaluates the offer and haggles over any specifics that are required, like start date, benefits, and compensation.

The following advice can help you better grasp the interview process and raise your chances of success:

1. Do some research on the role and the firm. This will demonstrate your interest in the position and help you respond to inquiries effectively.
2. Be ready to answer typical interview questions. You can prepare for frequently

asked interview questions with the aid of a plethora of online and print materials.

3. Answer questions aloud to a friend or relative, or practice in front of a mirror. You'll feel more at ease and assured throughout the interview if you do this.
4. Make sure you appear on time for your interview and dress professionally.
5. Treat everybody you experience with kindness and regard.
6. When the interview is about to end, ask questions. This shows your advantage in the position and the association.
7. Up-and-comers can work on their odds of coming out on top and getting their optimal occupation by monitoring the screening and planning fittingly.

Breakdown of the various stages of the interview process

Inspecting the screening comprehensively uncovers the means and huge parts that structure the expansion between a competitor and their possible future chief. We will slow down the separating this part and arrange a thorough aide for completing each step with progress.

1. Beginning screening interview

Most managers direct fundamental meetings to get chosen candidates and guarantee their abilities are a sufficient counterpart for the job. In the event that an association is rethinking enrolling to an office, an outer scout will assume control over the underlying screening interviews. These underlying screening interviews are kept short, by and large a 15 brief telephone interview or through a video conferencing instrument. Screening interviews intend to limit which possibility to welcome to the authority's first meeting round.

Subsequently, common screening inquiries questions will be moderately broad, straight-forward, and pointed toward evaluating an up-and-comer's hard abilities and work insight. What pragmatic experience and abilities do they need to play out the gig possibly?

At this phase of the screening, you shouldn't zero in a lot on social fit and culture add yet. Rather, consider it as seeing whether the applicant "on paper" meets the necessities of the gig.

2. First meeting

The following stage in the screening is by and large alluded to as the main meeting. The main meeting is normally a one-on-one meeting with the candidate and recruiting chief. Regularly, the main meeting is face to face and on location, however it can likewise be a virtual or a phone interview.

The motivation behind a first meeting is to additionally evaluate the competitor's insight and capabilities by building further on the underlying screening.

The most well-known questions asked in a first meeting relate to the capabilities an organization is searching for in their ideal up-and-comer. The questioner will ask about the candidate's work history, experience, and abilities to decide if an up-and-comer can finish the work and fit in with the organization culture.

At this stage, you need to plunge a piece further into their experience, past what's written in their CV. At this point, you likewise may begin getting to realize the individual a piece better and in addition to their capabilities. You will develop this further during the subsequent stage in the screening.

3. Second meeting

Competitors welcomed briefly interview are serious competitors for the job. Frequently this round is where up-and-comers meet with various division heads and visit the work environment (when directed face to face). In the subsequent meeting, the employing director from the principal round may be available close by somebody who might straightforwardly work with the competitor.

The reason for the subsequent meeting is to additionally get to realize the competitor's work insight, yet additionally to begin surveying on the off chance that they are a decent social fit.

Second round inquiries questions are a profound jump into the points examined in the principal round. The examiner will routinely focus on work express requests that anticipate that competitors should reply with organized answers with unequivocal occasions of how their abilities will engage them to perform well in the gig.

Thusly, this round commonly incorporates conduct and situational questions:

Conduct questions request that up-and-comers review an encounter, make sense of how they dealt with it, and depict the result. They urge contender to share stories that detail where they succeeded or battled at past positions.

Situational questions present newcomers with theoretical conditions and ask them how they would reply. Such requests give information into a contender's decisive abilities to reason and how they handle workplace battle. Evaluating the answers for these requests will help with framing the last candidate list.

Various kinds of second requests test further into why the contender needs the work and the sum they know about or appreciate what the association does.

Right now, you should have obtained areas of strength for any of the promising newcomer's work knowledge and leaned toward ways to deal with working.

You've likewise got to know their character a smidgen more, providing you with a thought of whether they'd squeeze into your group.

You nearly completed the screening and tracked down your next enlist. In any case, prior to pursuing a choice, you should welcome the possibility for another meeting.

4. Third meeting

Not all screenings incorporate the third meeting, so what occurs in this round could happen in the subsequent meeting. At times, the third meeting happens after an up-and-comer has finished a task or could comprise a competitor show.

On the off chance that there is a third meeting, the objective will be to go significantly more profound into a competitor's capacity and fitness for the gig. This interview step will incorporate more social and situational questions. At this stage, you additionally need to pose any further inquiries you could need to evaluate how they could squeeze into your work environment culture and group structure.

These inquiries are totally asked in view of the up-and-comer being employed. They are speculative circumstances of what working with the applicant could resemble and how they could squeeze into your group.

5. The choice

At this stage, you shouldn't have multiple or two potential applicants left. The two players have gotten numerous opportunities to ask however many inquiries as they like, so any competitor that is passed on ought to make an extraordinary expansion to your group. So now is the ideal time to settle on the last choice.

The screening is finished once a deal is made to a competitor. Contingent upon the business, a few organizations do a record verification or contact references prior to sending an authority offer letter.

It's normal for possibility to initially get a verbal proposal via telephone or recorded as a hard copy by means of email (or both) to ensure they are content with the terms or recognize regions that need arranging.

When they acknowledge the proposition, you can authoritatively close the screening and the up-and-comer will continue on toward the following stage: the onboarding system.

Insight into common interview formats (phone, video, in-person) and what to expect

In the present multi-layered work market, interviews come in different arrangements, each with its remarkable elements and contemplations. Grasping the subtleties of telephone, video, and in-person meets is significant for effectively exploring the assorted scenes of the recruiting system.

1. Phone Interviews: A Preliminary Connection
   - Format: Typically, phone interviews serve as an initial screening phase.
   - What to Expect:
     - Brief, focused conversations with a recruiter or hiring manager.

- Questions aimed at assessing your qualifications, experience, and initial fit for the role.
- An opportunity to showcase your communication skills, enthusiasm, and interest in the position.

2. Video Interviews: Navigating the Virtual Realm

- Format: With the rise of remote work, video interviews have become increasingly common.
- What to Expect:
  - Interaction with interviewers via platforms like Zoom, Skype, or other video conferencing tools.
  - Similar questions as in in-person interviews, with a focus on how you present yourself virtually.
  - Potential technical aspects, such as ensuring a stable internet connection and familiarity with video conferencing tools.

3. In-Person Interviews: Making a Lasting Impression
- Format: Traditional face-to-face interviews remain a staple in the hiring process.
- What to Expect:
    - Meetings with hiring managers, team members, or a combination of both.
    - A comprehensive assessment of your interpersonal skills, body language, and overall professionalism.
    - Opportunities to tour the workplace, meet potential colleagues, and gain insights into company culture.

Tips for Success Across Formats:

Prepare Thoroughly: Research the company, understand the role, and be ready to articulate your qualifications.

Practice, Practice, Practice: Conduct mock interviews, especially for video scenarios, to familiarize yourself with the format.

Dress Appropriately: Whether in-person or virtual, present yourself professionally and in alignment with the company culture.

Engage in Active Listening: Pay close attention to questions, and provide thoughtful, relevant responses.

Highlight Adaptability: Showcase your ability to adapt to different interview formats, signaling flexibility in a dynamic work environment.

Understanding the unique characteristics of each interview format positions you to navigate the hiring process successfully. From the initial phone call to the virtual or in-person meeting, being well-prepared and adaptable ensures you can confidently present your best self, regardless of the format.

CHAPTER 2: Crafting Your Personal Brand

In the cutthroat scene of the expert world, standing apart goes past a heavenly resume and great certifications. Your own image is the interesting account that separates you, exhibiting your abilities as well as your character, values, and the unmistakable worth you offer of real value. We should dig into the specialty of making an individual brand that reverberates with legitimacy and has an enduring effect.

Developing a compelling personal brand that aligns with the job market

A convincing individual brand is one that is interesting, real, and lined up with the gig market. It is a method for separating yourself from different competitors and showing potential bosses why you are the most qualified individual.

To foster a convincing individual brand, you ought to:

1. Recognize your extraordinary offer. What makes you not the same as different up-and-comers? What are your assets, abilities, and interests? What one of a kind viewpoint do you offer that might be of some value?

2. Characterize your interest group. Who are you attempting to reach with your own image? What organizations or businesses would you say you are generally keen on?

When you know your main interest group, you can fit your informing and marking components to speak to them.

3. Make an individual brand proclamation. This is a brief and significant explanation that sums up your extraordinary incentive and what you bring to the table. It would be ideal for it to be clear, brief, and simple to recollect.

4. Curate your internet based presence. Your internet based presence is in many cases the principal thing potential bosses will see, so establishing a decent connection is significant. Ensure your virtual entertainment profiles, site, and other internet based resources are proficient and mirror your own image.

5. Network with others in your field. Go to industry occasions, associate

with individuals on LinkedIn, and contact individuals you respect for enlightening meetings. Organizing is an extraordinary method for building connections, finding out about new open doors, and advancing your own image.

Here are a few ways to adjust your own image to the gig market:

Research the organizations and ventures you are keen on. What are their qualities? What are their objectives? What are they searching for in applicants?

Tailor your own image to engage your main interest group. For instance, on the off chance that you are going after a position at a tech startup, you should underline your inventive reasoning and your capacity to work rapidly and proficiently.

Use catchphrases that are pertinent to the gig market in your resume, introductory letter, and online profiles. This will assist you with getting seen by potential managers who are utilizing candidate global positioning frameworks (ATS).

Feature your abilities and experience that are generally pertinent to the positions you are applying for. Make certain to measure your achievements whenever the situation allows.

Get criticism from others on your own image. Ask your companions, family, and partners their thought process of your own image explanation and your web-based presence. Their input can assist you with working on your own image and make it more lined up with the gig market.

By fostering a convincing individual brand that is lined up with the gig market, you can build your odds of coming out on top in your pursuit of employment.

Creating a strong online presence and leveraging social media for professional visibility

In the computerized age, your web-based presence is a window into your expert world. Making a vigorous web-based persona and tackling the force of online entertainment can fundamentally improve your expert perceivability, opening ways to open doors and laying out you as an ideal chief in your field. We should investigate how to construct and use your internet based presence decisively.

1. Advance Your LinkedIn Profile:

Proficient Headshot and Convincing Title:

Transfer an expert photograph and art a convincing title that briefly portrays your skill.

Itemized Synopsis and Experience:

Compose a far reaching rundown and detail your work insight, stressing key accomplishments and abilities.

Supports and Proposals:

Look for support and proposals from associates and managers to fabricate validity.

2. Take part in Industry-Significant Stages:
Pick Your Foundation Admirably:
Distinguish stages applicable to your industry. LinkedIn is an unquestionable necessity, yet consider others like Twitter, Instagram, or industry-explicit discussions.
Share Bits of knowledge and Content:
Consistently share industry experiences, articles, or your own substance to exhibit your insight and enthusiasm.
Draw in with others by remarking and taking part in conversations.
3. Make and Offer Substance:
Begin a Blog or Compose Articles:
Share your skill by beginning a blog or composing articles on stages like Medium or LinkedIn.
Position yourself as an idea chief by offering significant experiences and answers for industry challenges.

4. Build a Professional Website or Portfolio:

Centralized Hub for Your Work:

Create a personal website or portfolio showcasing your professional journey, projects, and achievements.

Incorporate connections to your web-based entertainment profiles, making it simple for others to associate with you.

5. Network Actively:

Connect with Professionals:

Actively connect with professionals in your industry. Personalize connection requests to foster meaningful connections.

Join and participate in industry-specific groups and forums to expand your network.

6. Showcase Your Personality:

Balancing Professionalism and Personality:

Share aspects of your personality while maintaining professionalism.

Humanize your online presence by sharing relevant personal insights, hobbies, or behind-the-scenes moments.

7. Participate in Webinars and Online Events:

Be a Visible Presence:

Attend and participate in webinars and virtual events within your industry.

Share your takeaways and engage with speakers and attendees on social media.

8. Monitor Your Online Reputation:

Google Yourself:

Regularly Google your name to monitor your online presence.

Address any inaccuracies or inconsistencies and ensure that your digital footprint aligns with your professional brand.

9. Stay Consistent:

Unified Branding Across Platforms:

Keep a reliable brand picture across the entirety of your web-based stages.

Use the same professional photo, headline, and bio to ensure uniformity.

10. Seek Professional Development Opportunities:

Online Courses and Certifications:

Highlight ongoing professional development by sharing certificates and accomplishments from online courses.

Exhibit your obligation to remaining current in your field.

Building serious areas of strength for a presence isn't just about having a profile; it's about decisively organizing a computerized story that lines up with your expert objectives. By effectively captivating in web-based networks, sharing significant substance, and displaying your one of a kind experiences, you can use online entertainment as an integral asset for proficient perceivability and professional success.

CHAPTER 3: Preparing for Success

Success rarely happens by chance; it's often the result of careful planning, preparation, and a commitment to excellence. Whether you're gearing up for a project, a career move, or a personal goal, the process of preparation is key to achieving the outcomes you desire. Let's explore a strategic approach to preparing for success.

1. Set Clear Objectives:

Define Your Goals:

Clearly articulate what success looks like for you. What are your objectives, and what do you hope to achieve?

Break down overarching goals into smaller, actionable steps for a more manageable approach.

2. Research and Gather Information:

- Informed Decision-Making:
    - Conduct thorough research related to your goals. Whether it's a project, job change, or personal endeavor, gather relevant information.
    - Keep awake to-date with industry patterns and experiences to pursue informed choices.

3. Create a Plan of Action:
    - Strategic Roadmap:
        - Develop a detailed plan outlining the steps you need to take to reach your goals.
        - Establish timelines, milestones, and deadlines to stay on track.

4. Invest in Skill Development:
    - Continuous Learning:
        - Identify the skills required for success in your chosen area.
        - Invest time and resources in learning and honing these skills to enhance your capabilities.

5. Build a Support System:

Surround Yourself with Positivity:

Cultivate a network of supportive individuals who can offer guidance and encouragement.

Seek mentorship and connect with like-minded individuals who share your aspirations.

6. Focus on Using time effectively:

Successful Time Distribution:

Focus on errands in view of their significance and direness.

Embrace time usage strategies to amplify efficiency and limit pressure.

7. Embrace Versatility:

Adaptability in Approach:

Perceive that plans might require change en route.

Embrace versatility and be available to refine your methodology in view of developing conditions.

8. Develop a Positive Mentality:

Positive thinking Powers Achievement:

Encourage a positive outlook and have confidence in your capacity to accomplish your objectives.

Address difficulties with an answer situated outlook, seeing them as any open doors for development.

9. Picture Achievement:

Mental Practice:

Imagine your prosperity consistently. Envisioning positive results can support your responsibility and inspiration.

Use certifications and mental practice to construct trust in your abilities.

10. Assess and Change:

Consistent Improvement:

Routinely evaluate your advancement against your goals.

Change your arrangement, gain from encounters, and ceaselessly refine your methodology.

11. Observe Achievements:

Recognize Accomplishments:

Celebrate more modest triumphs en route. Recognizing progress lifts inspiration and confidence level.
Consider your excursion and perceive the means you've taken toward progress.

Getting ready for progress isn't just about the outcome; about developing a mentality and approach expands your expected route. By setting clear goals, remaining versatile, and putting resources into ceaseless learning, you position yourself for outcome in your undertakings. Keep in mind, achievement isn't an objective yet an excursion of development, learning, and accomplishment.

Research strategies for understanding the company and the role

While you're talking with a task, understanding the organization and the job however much as could be expected is significant.

This will help you with answering inquiries astutely, display your benefit in the position, and show that you're great for the gathering.

The following are a couple of assessment strategies for getting a handle on the association and the work:

1. Visit the association site. This is a phenomenal spot to learn about the association's arrangement of encounters, mission, vision, values, things or organizations, and target market. You can in like manner track down information about the association's lifestyle, benefits, and work open doors.

2. Scrutinize the association's blog and electronic diversion posts. This will give you a sensation of what the association is doing, what they're vivacious about, and how they interface with their clients and delegates.

3. Look for reports and reviews about the association. This can give you pieces of information into the association's standing, its show watching out, and its workplace culture.

4. Talk with people who work at the association. Expecting you to realize any person who works at the association, get some data about their experience. They can give you pieces of information into the association culture, the gathering components, and the solicitations of the gig.

5. Examine work postings for relative positions. This can give you a sensation of the capacities and experience that organizations are looking for.

6. Research the association's adversaries. This will help you with understanding the association's circumstance keeping watch and the challenges that it faces.

7. Research the genuine work. What are the ordinary commitments of the gig? What capacities and experience are required? What are the hardships and chances of the gig? The more you recognize the work, the more prepared you'll be to resolve questions and show your fit for the position.

By following these assessment techniques, you can get a significant cognizance of the association and the work. This will help you with laying out a respectable association during the screening and augmentation of your potential outcomes getting enlisted.

Here are a few extra tips:
Be coordinated. Monitor your exploration discoveries in a bookkeeping sheet or journal.

This will assist you with effectively referring to the data during the screening.

Be specific. Not everything research is made equivalent. Center around tracking down valid wellsprings of data.

Be basic. Really try not to take all that you read at face respect. Question the data and structure your own perspective.

Be ready to discuss your exploration. During the meeting, be prepared to discuss what you found out about the organization and the job. Be explicit and give models.

By following these tips, you can lead viable exploration and gain a profound comprehension of the organization and the job. This will assist you with acing your meeting and land the most amazing job you could ever ask for.

Developing a tailored approach to common interview questions

Many interview questions are normal, however that doesn't mean you ought to give canned replies. Managers can recognize a nonexclusive response well in advance. All things considered, get some margin to fit your solutions to each meet with and to feature your extraordinary abilities and experience.

- Here are a ways to foster a fitted way to deal with normal inquiries questions:
- Contemplate what the business is truly inquiring about. What are they attempting to find out about you with this question? When you understand what they're searching for, you can tailor your solution to exhibit that you have the right stuff and experience they're chasing.
- Utilize explicit guides to help your responses. Try not to simply let the questioner know that you're a diligent

employee and a cooperative person. Show them by sharing explicit instances of times when you exhibited these characteristics.

Be brief and direct. Businesses lack the opportunity to pay attention to long, meandering responses. Arrive at the point rapidly and obviously.

Practice your responses. The more you practice, the more certain and clean you'll sound during the meeting.

Here are some examples of how to tailor your answers to common interview questions:

Question: Tell me about yourself.

Generic answer: I'm a diligent employee and I'm continuously ready to learn new things. I'm likewise a cooperative person and I'm continuously ready to assist my partners.

Tailored answer: I'm a computer programmer with 5 years of involvement with creating and keeping up with web applications. I'm enthusiastic about building great items that address the issues of clients. I'm likewise major areas of strength for an and I'm ready to work really with both specialized and non-specialized partners.

Question: For what reason would you say you are keen on this position?

Generic answer: I'm keen on this position since it's an extraordinary chance to utilize my abilities and experience to have an effect.

Tailored answer: I'm keen on this position since I'm enthusiastic about creating imaginative items that work on individuals' lives. I'm likewise amped up for the valuable chance to work with a group of skilled designers and to gain from probably simply incredible.

Question: What are your assets and shortcomings?

Generic answer: My assets are that I'm a diligent employee and I'm continuously ready to learn new things. My shortcomings are that I can be somewhat of a stickler and I once in a while experience difficulty designating undertakings.

Tailored answer: One of my assets is my capacity to rapidly learn new advances and to apply them to tackle genuine issues. I'm likewise ready to work freely and as a feature of a group to accomplish shared objectives. One of my shortcomings is that I can be somewhat of a fussbudget and I sometimes experience difficulty relinquishing errands. Notwithstanding, I'm dealing with this and I'm figuring out how to trust my colleagues to take care of business.

By following these tips, you can develop a tailored approach to common interview questions. This will assist you with establishing a decent connection with bosses and increment your possibilities of getting employed.

CHAPTER 4: Mastering the Art of Self-Promotion

Self-promotion is the specialty of imparting your abilities, experience, and achievements to others in a positive and powerful manner. It is a fundamental expertise for progress in any field, yet it is particularly significant in the present serious work market.

Here are some tips for mastering the art of self-promotion:

1. Be clear about your incentive. What makes you remarkable and important? What do you bring to the table that others don't? When you realize your offer, you can impart it to others in a reasonable and brief manner.

2. Be valid. Individuals can detect a phony well in advance, so act naturally and let your character

radiate through. Do whatever it takes not to endeavor to be another person.

3. Be explicit. Try not to simply let individuals know that you're a diligent employee or that you're a cooperative person. Show them by sharing explicit instances of your abilities and experience.

4. Be positive. Center around your assets and achievements. Try not to harp on your shortcomings or disappointments.

5. Be sure. Put stock in yourself and your capacities. Certainty is infectious, so when you project certainty, others will have faith in you as well.

Here are some specific ways to promote yourself:

Network with others. Go to industry occasions, associate with individuals on LinkedIn, and contact individuals you respect for enlightening meetings. Organizing is an incredible method for getting your name out there and to fabricate associations with expected businesses, clients, and teammates.

Share your mastery. Compose blog entries, articles, and digital books. Give introductions at industry occasions. Record recordings and offer them via online entertainment. Sharing your mastery is an extraordinary method for setting up a good foundation for yourself as an ideal chief in your field and to stand out from expected bosses and clients.

Advance your work. At the point when you complete a task or accomplish an objective, share it with your organization. You can do this via online entertainment, in your email signature, or in your resume. Advancing your work is an incredible method for getting seen and to construct your standing.

Get tributes and proposals. Ask your clients, partners, and administrators to compose tributes and suggestions for you. Tributes and proposals are an incredible method for showing possible businesses and clients that you are a significant resource.

By following these tips, you can become amazing at self-advancement and increment your odds of coming out on top in your vocation.

Here are a few extra tips:

Be aware of your crowd. Tailor your self-advancement messages to the particular individuals you are attempting to reach.

Be reliable. Self-advancement is definitely not a one-time occasion. It is a continuous interaction.

Be predictable with your self-advancement endeavors and you will get results over the long haul.

Show restraint. It requires investment to fabricate a standing and to draw in valuable open doors. Do whatever it takes not to get hindered if you don't move results immediately. Simply continue to put yourself out there and you will ultimately accomplish your objectives.

Self-advancement is a fundamental expertise for progress in any field. By becoming amazing at self-advancement, you can build your possibilities of getting recruited, getting advanced, and accomplishing your vocation objectives.

Techniques for confidently showcasing your skills and achievements

Confidently showcasing your skills and achievements is a key aspect of professional success. Whether in job interviews, performance reviews, or networking events, effectively communicating your value requires a blend of self-assurance and strategic communication. Here are techniques to help you confidently highlight your skills and achievements:

Know Your Stuff:

Start by making a list of all the things you're good at, both the technical stuff and the soft skills.

Keep updating this list as you learn and grow.

Tell a Story:

When you're talking about what you've done, think of it like telling a story.

- Share experiences that show how you used your skills to overcome challenges or make things happen.

Use the CAR Method (Challenge, Action, Result):

- Talk about the problems or challenges you faced (Challenge).
- Share what you did to fix it (Action).
- Finish with the positive results you achieved (Result).

Put Numbers on It:

- Add some numbers to your achievements. Percentages, timeframes, anything that makes it more concrete.
- It helps people see the real impact of what you've done.

Communicate in Their Language:

- Tailor your message to your crowd. What do they care about? What matters to them?
- Highlight the skills and achievements that matter most in that context.

Look Confident, Even If You're Nervous:

Pay attention to how you carry yourself. Look people in the eye, use your hands to emphasize points, and stand tall.

Even if you're nervous inside, a confident posture can make a big difference.

Practice, Practice, Practice:

Practice talking about your skills and achievements. Do it before a mirror or with a companion.

Positive self-talk helps too. Remind yourself of your successes regularly.

Show Some Proof:

Create a portfolio with examples of your work, projects, or anything you're proud of.

It's a great visual aid for discussions about your skills.

Transferable Skills Matter:

Highlight skills that work in different situations. Show that you're adaptable.

It makes you versatile and ready for anything.

Ask Yourself, "So What?":

When talking about something, ask yourself, "So what?" Make sure your message has real relevance and impact.

Be Enthusiastic:

Let your excitement about your work shine through.

Passion is contagious, and people appreciate someone who loves what they do.

Learn from Feedback:

Ask for feedback from mentors or friends on how you talk about your skills.

Use their insights to get better at it.

Stay Updated:

Regularly update your skills list to reflect what you're currently rocking.

Be ready to chat about your recent achievements.

Own Your Success:

Don't shy away from acknowledging your successes. Own them with confidence.

You've worked hard for it; don't be afraid to share it.

Connect Skills to the Future:

Relate your skills and achievements to what you want to do next.

Show that you're not just awesome in the past; you're ready for more in the future.

So, when you're talking about yourself, remember you're not bragging; you're just confidently sharing your story. It's about letting people know what you bring to the table and how you're ready to make things happen.

Crafting effective and memorable elevator pitches

An elevator pitch is a brief summary of your skills, experience, and goals that you can deliver in the amount of time it takes to ride an elevator (about 30-60 seconds). It is an incredible method for acquainting yourself with expected managers, clients, and different experts.

To craft an effective and memorable elevator pitch, follow these tips:

Start with a strong hook. The initial couple of moments of your short presentation are basic. You need to grab the listener's attention and make them want to learn more. You can do this by starting with a strong hook, such as a surprising statistic, a provocative question, or a compelling story.

Be clear and concise. Get to the point quickly and clearly. Don't overload your elevator pitch with too much information. Center around the most significant and important focuses.

Highlight your unique value proposition.What makes you not quite the same as others in your field? For what reason ought individuals think often about you and what you bring to the table? Make sure your elevator pitch highlights your unique value proposition.

Use strong action verbs. When describing your skills and experience, use strong action verbs to show what you have accomplished. Be enthusiastic. Show the listener that you are passionate about what you do. Be enthusiastic and excited about your elevator pitch.

Here is an illustration of a compelling short presentation:

I am a software engineer with 5 years of experience in developing and maintaining web applications. I am passionate about building high-quality products that meet the needs of users. I'm likewise serious areas of strength for an and I'm ready to work successfully with both specialized and non-specialized partners.

This elevator pitch is effective because it:

Starts with a strong hook: "I am a software engineer with 5 years of experience..."

Is clear and concise: The elevator pitch gets to the point quickly and clearly, and only includes the most important and relevant information.

Highlights a unique value proposition: The elevator pitch highlights the speaker's passion for building high-quality products that meet the needs of users, as well as their strong communication and collaboration skills.

Uses strong action verbs: The elevator pitch uses strong action verbs to describe the speaker's skills and experience, such as "developing and maintaining web applications" and "working effectively with both technical and non-technical stakeholders."

Is enthusiastic: The elevator pitch is enthusiastic and shows that the speaker is passionate about what they do.

To practice your elevator pitch, try delivering it to a friend, family member, or colleague. Ask them for feedback on how you can improve your delivery and make your pitch more effective.

By following these tips, you can craft an elevator pitch that is effective, memorable, and will help you achieve your career goals.

CHAPTER 5: Building a Winning Resume

A winning resume is one that is clear, brief, and custom fitted to the particular work you are applying for. It ought to feature your abilities and involvement in a way that is simple for expected bosses to peruse and comprehend.

Here are a few methods for building a winning resume:

1. Begin with areas of strength for an outline or goal. This is your opportunity to let potential managers know what your identity is, what you do, and what you're searching for in a task. Ensure your rundown or goal is clear, brief, and custom fitted to the gig you're applying for.

2. Feature your abilities and experience. List your abilities and involvement with switch sequential requests, with your latest work

first. Make certain to incorporate your work title, organization name, and dates of work for each work. Additionally, list your vital abilities and achievements for each work.

3. Use watchwords all through your resume. At the point when potential bosses look for up-and-comers, they frequently use watchwords to limit their query items. Try to incorporate important watchwords all through your resume, particularly in your synopsis or goal and in your abilities and experience segment.

4. Tailor your resume to every occupation you apply for. Set aside some margin to fit your resume to each occupation you apply for. This implies featuring the abilities and experience that are generally pertinent to the gig you're applying for.

5. Edit cautiously. Make a point to edit your resume cautiously prior to submitting it to possible businesses. Mistakes and syntactic blunders can make you look

amateurish and can hurt your possibilities of getting employed.

Here are a few extra methods for building a winning resume:

Utilize a straightforward and simple-to-understand textual style.

Utilize a blank area to make your resume simple to filter.

Utilize strong and italics to feature significant data.

Use list items to list your abilities and experience.

Measure your achievements whenever the situation allows.

Utilize solid activity action words.

Get criticism from others on your resume.

By following these tips, you can build a winning resume that will help you land your dream job.

Here is an illustration of a solid resume rundown:

Software engineer with 5 years of experience in developing and maintaining web applications. Demonstrated capacity to work freely and as a component of a group to convey great items on time and inside spending plans. Expertise in Java, Python, and SQL.

This summary is effective because it:

Is clear and concise.

Highlights the applicant's skills and experience in a relevant way.

Uses keywords that are relevant to many software engineering jobs.

Shows that the applicant is a team player and is able to deliver results.

By following these tips, you can write a resume that will help you stand out from the competition and land your dream job.

Tips for creating a resume that stands out to potential employers

In various ways, a resume is the main push toward your future calling, as it's by and large the essential thing a selecting boss sees. It implies a lot to lay out a good association by presenting an unblemished and minimal resume that nuances your capacities for the open work.

A resume is a report that shows a contender's capacities for an undertaking. Much of the time integrates their tutoring, experience, capacities and achievements. A resume is a phenomenal method for displaying how you could be an asset for the association. Having a cleaned procedure is an uncommon strategy for isolating yourself from various contenders pursuing a comparable position. While making a resume, it's moreover basic to fathom the business you're working in as well as the enlisting association you're applying to tailor your resume to both.

There are numerous approaches to isolating your resume from the rest. What a spotter looks for will extraordinarily depend upon your industry and the work you're applying for, but, generally speaking, selecting bosses search proceeds with that stick out. Coming up next are a couple of clues to consider while making your resume:

1. Grasp what the enlisting chief is looking for
Before you begin making your resume, review the work posting and the association's site. Take careful thought while sorting out what you plan to consolidate. Center around the organization's way of life, watchwords you need to incorporate and what's generally anticipated of you in this job.

2. Tailor it to your industry and the work you're applying for
Make sure to integrate center around business experience that displays relevant capacities. If you're pursuing a situation as a writer, the selecting boss would help more from being known all about your capacities as a school journalist than as a sitter. Incorporate just

significant places that let your future business in on you comprehend what they're searching for in a representative.

3. Incorporate a header and synopsis or goal

Scouts survey a huge volume of resumes every day. Counting a header and synopsis or goal can help recruiting supervisors notice your resume among others. While adding a header, ensure your name is at the extreme top. Assuming that you have space, make the text dimension somewhat bigger. Incorporate your location (or just city and state), telephone number and email address. Incorporate contact data where the employing supervisor is probably going to contact you.

Right underneath your header, compose a synopsis or goal. A synopsis is no longer than three sentences and surveys your important experience and abilities. A goal makes sense of your profession objective and what abilities you can bring to the organization. It's something like two sentences. Counting one of these assertions sums up your resume at the top so employing supervisors can survey it and find out about you rapidly.

4. Add appropriate abilities

Very much like with your past positions, just incorporate abilities that would be significant to the position you're applying for. Check the work posting for abilities or necessities that the employing supervisor is searching for. For instance, posting your insight into plan programming and projects would be significant abilities to incorporate while going after a visual computerization job.

5. Keep it succinct

While a resume can be two pages, most ought to be only one. This is much of the time the case for passage level applicants with negligible experience. As you draft your resume, ensure you're just including data that could be useful to you in contrast to the opposition. Keep away from overt repetitiveness and cushion.

6. Make it outwardly engaging

While selection representatives will see the value in a very much planned continuation, ensure your imagination is proficient. The following are a couple of interesting points while planning a cutting edge continue:

Text style: Ensure the textual style you use is intelligible. Utilize an expert text style like Georgia, Times New Roman, Calibri or Helvetica.

Text dimension: Picking a fittingly measured text style will guarantee an enrollment specialist's capacity to peruse the substance of your resume. Size 12 text style ought to do the trick.

Template: Keep your plans negligible and stylishly engaging. In the event that you're utilizing a layout, ensure the visual components don't occupy from the substance of your resume.

Variety decisions: Utilize an appealing variety while planning your resume. Decide on dark, white and a third variety like blue or green. White is an incredible foundation tone, dark is best for text and your third tone can feature significant subtleties on your resume.

On the off chance that you're going after an inventive position, your resume is the main example of your plan work that scouts will see. Ensure you show your special style. Having a perfect and decipherable resume will guarantee their capacity to pursue it completely without disarray or interruption.

7. Present an introductory letter

At the point when businesses have you present a resume on the web, they could ask you for an introductory letter too. Regardless of whether it's not needed, sending an introductory letter is an incredible method for standing apart as an up-and-comer. On the off chance that you do, ensure the plan and variety plan of your introductory letter matches that of your resume for a more firm look.

8. Edit

Make a point to edit your resume prior to submitting it. A mistake free and simple to-peruse continues shows your amazing skill and your capacity to give close consideration to detail. On the off chance that you tailor your resume to each position you apply for, try to painstakingly peruse it each time, or ask a confidant companion or relative to survey it for you.

Aligning your resume with the job description and company culture

Aligning your resume to the set of working responsibilities and company culture is fundamental for expanding your possibilities of getting recruited. Thus, you show potential bosses that you are the most qualified individual that you are ideal for their organization.

Here are a few ways to adjust your resume to the set of working responsibilities and company culture:

1. Painstakingly read and investigate the set of working responsibilities.

Begin by completely perusing and dissecting the expected set of responsibilities. Focus on the language and tone utilized in the portrayal, as it can give important experiences into the organization's requirements and assumptions.

2. Distinguish the vital abilities and prerequisites.

When you have a decent comprehension of the set of working responsibilities, recognize the critical abilities and prerequisites that the business is searching for. Make a point to feature these abilities and prerequisites in your resume.

3. Use catchphrases all through your resume.

Utilize the very watchwords that are utilized as part of the set of working responsibilities all through your resume. This will assist your resume with being gotten by candidate global positioning frameworks (ATS) and will show potential bosses that you have the right stuff and experience they are searching for.

4. Tailor your resume to the organization culture.

Research the organization culture and values. Attempt to comprehend what the organization is energetic about and what it values in its representatives. You can do this by perusing the organization's site, web-based entertainment pages, and blog entries. When you have a decent comprehension of the organization culture, tailor your resume to feature the abilities and experience that are generally pertinent to the organization culture.

5. Feature your achievements.

While portraying your abilities and experience, make certain to feature your achievements. Utilize explicit models and measure your outcomes whenever the situation allows. This will assist likely bosses with seeing the worth that you can bring to their organization.

6. Edit cautiously.

Prior to presenting your resume to expected bosses, make certain to painstakingly edit it. Mistakes and syntactic blunders can make you look amateurish and can hurt your possibilities of getting employed.

Here is an illustration of how to adjust your resume to the expected set of responsibilities and company culture:

Expected set of responsibilities:

We are searching for a programmer with 5 years of involvement with creating and keeping up with web applications. The ideal up-and-comer will have major areas of strength for any of Java, Python, and SQL. Moreover, the ideal up-and-comer will be a cooperative person and will actually want to work freely to convey excellent items on time and inside spending plans.

Organization culture:

Our organization is energetic about building imaginative and easy to understand items. We esteem cooperation, inventiveness, and an uplifting outlook.

Resume:

Summary:

Computer programmer with 5 years of involvement with creating and keeping up with web applications. Demonstrated capacity to work freely and as a component of a group to convey top notch items on time and inside spending plan. Mastery in Java, Python, and SQL.

Skills:

Java

Python
SQL
Web improvement
Collaboration
Critical thinking
Imagination
Experience:
Programmer
Summit Company
2020 - Present
Created and kept up with web applications utilizing Java, Python, and SQL
Worked with a group of specialists to convey top notch items on time and inside spending plan
Effectively sent off a few new web applications that have been generally welcomed by clients
Examination:
This resume is lined up with the expected set of responsibilities and company culture in more than one way:
The resume features the candidate's abilities and involvement with Java, Python, and SQL, which are the key qualities expected for the gig.

The resume utilizes watchwords all through, which will assist it with being gotten by candidate global positioning frameworks (ATS).

The resume features the candidate's capacity to work freely and as a component of a group, which is essential to the organization culture.

The resume gives explicit instances of the candidate's achievements, which shows their worth to the organization.

By following these tips, you can adjust your resume to the set of working responsibilities and company culture, which will expand your possibilities of getting recruited.

CHAPTER 6: Navigating Behavioral Interviews

Behavioral interviews are a type of job interview that spotlights on your past way of behaving and encounters to evaluate your fit for the job and the organization culture. Behavioral interview questions are typically structured around the STAR method, which stands for Situation, Task, Action, and Result.

Here are some additional tips for navigating behavioral interviews successfully:

> Be ready to discuss your disappointments. Everybody has their faults, and managers need to know how you gain from your disappointments. While responding to conduct inquiries, be ready to discuss when you committed an error and how you dealt with it. Make certain to zero in on what you gained from the experience

and how you would do things another way later on.

- Tailor your responses to the set of working responsibilities. While responding to social inquiries, make certain to fit your solutions to the particular set of working responsibilities you are talking with. Feature the abilities and experience that are generally pertinent to the gig and that show your fit for the job.
- Be brief and direct. Bosses are occupied individuals, so be compact and forthright in your responses. Try not to meander aimlessly or go off on digressions.
- Practice your responses. The more you work on addressing social inquiries, the more certain and clean you will sound during the meeting.

Here is an example of a behavioral interview question and how to answer it using the STAR method:

Question: Tell me about a time when you had to deal with conflict with a colleague.

Situation: I was working on a project with a colleague who had a different work style than me. We clashed on a number of issues, and it was difficult to get work done together.

Task: I needed to resolve the conflict and find a way to work effectively with my colleague.

Action: I approached my colleague and explained that I was having some difficulty working with them. We had a frank discussion about our different work styles and how we could better communicate and collaborate. We also agreed to set some ground rules for working together.

Result: After our discussion, we were able to resolve the conflict and work together more effectively. We had the option to finish the undertaking on time and to an exclusive requirement.

By following these tips, you can navigate behavioral interviews successfully and increase your chances of getting the job.

Understanding and responding to behavioral questions

Behavioral interview questions are designed to assess your soft skills, such as communication, problem-solving, teamwork, and leadership. They are typically structured around the STAR method, which stands for Situation, Task, Action, and Result.

To understand and respond to behavioral questions effectively, it is important to:

1. Identify the skill or competency that the question is assessing. The interviewer is trying

to learn more about your specific skills and experiences, so it is important to identify the skill or competency that the question is assessing. For example, if the question is "Tell me about a time when you had to deal with a difficult customer," the interviewer is trying to assess your customer service skills.

2. Think of a specific example that demonstrates the skill or competency. Once you have identified the skill or competency that the question is assessing, think of a specific example from your past that demonstrates that skill or competency. The example should be clear, concise, and relevant to the job you are interviewing for.

3. Utilize the STAR technique to structure your response. When answering the question, use the STAR method to structure your answer. This will help you to be clear and concise, and it will also help the interviewer to understand your thought process and how you approached the situation.

4. Be honest and authentic. Behavioral interview questions are designed to assess your true self, so it is important to be honest and authentic in your answers. Don't try to be someone you're not or to make up stories. The questioner needs to get to know the genuine you.

Here is an example of how to answer a behavioral question using the STAR method:

Question: Tell me about a time when you had to deal with a difficult customer.

Answer:

Situation: I was working as a retail cashier when a customer came in and was very upset about a product that they had purchased. They were yelling and screaming at me, and they were demanding a refund.

Task: I needed to calm the customer down and resolve the issue.

Action: I took the customer aside and apologized for their experience. I then listened to their concerns and explained the company's refund policy. I was able to offer the customer a partial refund, and they were satisfied with the outcome.

Result: The customer calmed down and left the store happy. I was able to resolve the issue without escalating the situation.

This answer is effective because it:

> Clearly identifies the skill or competency that the question is assessing (customer service skills)
>
> Provides a specific example from the past that demonstrates the skill or competency
>
> Uses the STAR method to structure the answer
>
> Is honest and authentic

By following these tips, you can understand and respond to behavioral questions effectively and increase your chances of getting the job.

Showcasing your experience through the STAR (Situation, Task, Action, Result) method

When discussing your experiences, particularly in interviews or professional conversations, using the STAR method can be highly effective. STAR stands for Situation, Task, Action, and Result – a structured approach that allows you to communicate your accomplishments and problem-solving skills clearly. Let's dive into each component of the STAR method:

**1. Situation:

Set the Stage:

Begin by outlining the context or situation you were in. What was the challenge or scenario?

Be concise but provide enough detail for the listener to understand the backdrop.

**2. Task:

Define Your Role:

Clearly articulate your role or task within the given situation. What were you responsible for?

Highlight any specific objectives or goals you need to achieve.

**3. Action:

Describe Your Actions:

Detail the specific actions you took to address the situation and accomplish the task.

Focus on your individual contributions, emphasizing your skills and decision-making process.

**4. Result:

Highlight the Outcome:

Share the positive outcomes or results of your actions. What happened as a direct result of your efforts?

Whenever possible, quantify the results to add measurable impact.

Let's break down the STAR method with an example:

Example:

Situation: During a tight deadline for a project delivery, our team faced a significant setback when a crucial team member unexpectedly fell ill.

Task: As the project manager, my task was to ensure that we not only met the deadline but also maintained the quality standards set by the client.

Action: I immediately reassessed the project timeline and redistributed tasks among the remaining team members. Simultaneously, I collaborated with the absent team member remotely to ensure a smooth transfer of their responsibilities. I also proactively communicate with the client, managing their expectations and providing a revised timeline.

Result: In spite of the underlying difficulty, we effectively conveyed the venture on time, satisfying every quality rule. The client esteemed our straightforwardness and proactive correspondence, provoking positive information and anticipated future composed endeavors. Likewise, the experience highlighted the meaning of comprehensively instructing inside the gathering to assuage chances related with unexpected aggravations.

Utilizing the STAR technique assists you with introducing your encounters in an organized and convincing way. It empowers you to feature your part in different circumstances as well as the substantial effect of your activities. Whether examining past accomplishments or critical thinking situations, integrating the STAR technique into your narrating improves clearness and reverberates with questioners or associates.

CHAPTER 7: Acing Technical and Case Interviews

To ace technical and case interviews, you should be ready to show your insight and abilities in various ways. Here are a few hints:

Technical interviews

- Hopefully look for a way to improve on your specialized abilities. Ensure you have serious areas of strength for any of the center ideas and abilities that are pertinent to the job you're talking with for. This might incorporate programming dialects, programming advancement procedures, information designs and calculations, or explicit innovations.

- Work on coding issues. Numerous specialized meetings will incorporate coding difficulties. Work on taking care of coding issues on the web or with companions and partners. This will assist you with getting quicker and more precise at taking care of issues under tension.

- Have the option to make sense of your code. As well as having the option to compose the right code, you ought to likewise have the option to clear up your code for the questioner. This shows that you comprehend your code and that you can convey your thoughts successfully.

- Be ready to respond to specialized questions. The questioner might pose you with specialized inquiries about your abilities and experience. Be ready to respond to these inquiries in an unmistakable and brief manner.

Case interviews

Comprehend the case screening. Case interviews are regularly organized with a particular goal in mind. The questioner will give you a business issue and request that you settle it. Be ready for this cycle and have a technique for moving toward case inquiries.

Have the option to think fundamentally and take care of issues. Case interviews are intended to evaluate your critical thinking abilities. Have the option to think basically and concoct savvy fixes to the issues that the questioner gives you.

Have the option to convey your perspective. The questioner needs to perceive how you approach issues and how you arrive at your decisions. Have the option to convey your point of view in a reasonable and succinct manner.

Be ready to seek clarification on some things. It's alright to pose inquiries during the case interview. This shows that you're locked in and that you're attempting to figure out the issue.

Here are some additional tips for acing technical and case interviews:

Be sure. Certainty is key in any meeting, however it's particularly significant in specialized and case interviews. The questioner needs to see that you have confidence in yourself and that you're equipped in every way necessary for the situation.

Be positive. Have an inspirational perspective and show the questioner that you're amped up for the open door.

Be ready. Work on noting normal specialized and case inquiries questions. This will assist you with feeling more certain and ready upon the arrival of the meeting.

By following these tips, you can build your possibilities acing specialized and case meetings and finding the most amazing job you could ever imagine.

Strategies for success in interviews that assess technical skills

To be successful in interviews that assess technical skills, you should be ready to show your insight and abilities in different ways. Here are a few methodologies that can assist you with succeeding:

Grasp the work necessities. The initial step is to painstakingly audit the expected set of responsibilities and distinguish the particular specialized abilities and information that are expected for the job. This will assist you with centering your planning endeavors and to guarantee that you are ready to respond to any inquiries that the questioner might pose.

Work on responding to normal specialized inquiries. There are various normal specialized inquiries questions that you can hope to be inquired about. Work on responding to these inquiries ahead of time with the goal that you can offer clear and brief responses during the meeting.

Have the option to make sense of your specialized ideas. As well as having the option to respond to explicit specialized questions, you ought to likewise have the option to clarify specialized ideas for the questioner in an unmistakable and brief manner. This exhibits how you might interpret the material and your capacity to really impart complex thoughts.

Have the option to tackle specialized issues. Numerous specialized meetings will incorporate coding difficulties or different kinds of specialized issues. Be ready to tackle these issues under tension and to make sense of your point of view for the questioner.

Have the option to investigate issues. The questioner may likewise ask you to investigate inquiries. Be ready to exhibit your capacity to distinguish and take care of specialized issues.

Here are a few extra tips for outcome in technical interviews:

Be sure. Certainty is key in any meeting, yet it is particularly significant in specialized interviews. The questioner needs to see that you have faith in yourself and that you are equipped for the situation.

Be ready to examine your activities. The questioner might request that you examine the specialized tasks that you have chipped away at previously. Be ready to portray your undertakings exhaustively and to feature your commitments.

Be ready to address social inquiries. Notwithstanding specialized questions, the questioner may likewise pose you social inquiries. Social inquiries are intended to evaluate your delicate abilities, for example, correspondence, critical thinking, and cooperation. Be ready to address conduct questions utilizing explicit models from quite a while ago.

By following these techniques, you can expand your odds of coming out on top in specialized meetings and land a truly amazing job.

Approaches to solving case studies and presenting solutions effectively

Case studies are a common interview format for business and consulting roles. They are intended to survey your critical thinking abilities, your capacity to think basically, and your capacity to successfully impart your thoughts.

To settle contextual analyses actually, follow these means:

- Explain the issue articulation. Ensure you comprehend the issue that you are being approached to settle. What is the particular inquiry that the questioner is posing? What are the limitations and suppositions?

- Recognize the central points of interest. When you grasp the issue articulation, distinguish the central points of contention that should be tended to. What are the main drivers of the issue? What are the various choices that you have for taking care of the issue?

Create and break down arrangements. Conceptualize a rundown of possible answers for the issue. Then, at that point, assess every arrangement in light of its practicality, viability, and cost.

Suggest an answer. Whenever you have assessed the likely arrangements as a whole, prescribe the best answer for the questioner. Make certain to make sense of your thinking and to legitimize your proposal.

To introduce your answer successfully, follow these tips:

Be clear and compact. Arrive at the point rapidly and try not to utilize language.

Be explicit. Give models and information to help your cases.

Be enticing. Make sense of why your answer is the best arrangement and how it will help the organization.

Be sure. Put stock in your answer and convey your show with certainty.

Here is an example of a case study:

Issue explanation: An organization is encountering a decrease in deals. The President believes you should foster an arrangement to increment deals.

Main points of contention:

The organization's items are obsolete.

The organization's showcasing system is ineffectual.

The organization's outreach group isn't performing great.

Solutions:

Foster new items that are more interesting to clients.

Execute another promoting methodology that spotlights via online entertainment and advanced showcasing.

Train the outreach group on new deals procedures.

Recommendation:

I suggest that the organization foster new items that are more interesting to clients. This is the most long haul arrangement and it will assist the organization with keeping an upper hand. The organization ought to likewise execute another advertising procedure that spotlights via online entertainment and computerized showcasing. This will assist the organization with contacting a more extensive crowd and to create more leads. At last, the organization ought to prepare the outreach group on new deals procedures. This will assist the deals with joining to be more viable in shutting bargains.

This is only one illustration of how to tackle a contextual investigation and present an answer successfully. The particular advances that you take and the way that you present your answer will differ contingent upon the particular contextual investigation and the questioner. By following the tips above, you can expand your odds of coming out on top in the event that you study interviews.

CHAPTER 8: Handling Common Interview Challenges

Here are some tips for handling common interview challenges:

Discussing yourself

Many individuals find it hard to discuss themselves in a positive light. In any case, it is critical to have the option to express your abilities, experience, and achievements in a reasonable and brief way during a meeting.

Here are a few hints:

Work on discussing yourself ahead of time. This will assist you with feeling more certain and ready upon the arrival of the meeting.

Center around your assets and achievements. Feature your most applicable abilities and experience for the job you are talking with for.

Be explicit and give models. Try not to simply let the questioner know that you are a decent communicator. Give them explicit instances of times when you have conveyed really.

Addressing troublesome inquiries

Questioners frequently pose troublesome inquiries to evaluate your critical thinking abilities and your capacity to basically think. Here are a few ways to respond to troublesome inquiries:

Pause for a minute to think before you reply. Try not to feel like you need to hurry into a response. Take a couple of seconds to contemplate the inquiry and to plan your reaction.

Tell the truth and bona fide. Try not to attempt to make up a response that you think the questioner needs to hear. Tell the truth and bona fide in your reaction.

Request explanation if necessary. In the event that you don't figure out an inquiry, request that the questioner explain it. This shows that you are locked in and that you need to completely grasp the inquiry.

Dealing with nerves

Feeling apprehensive during an interview is ordinary. Be that as it may, assuming your nerves are defeating you, performing well can be troublesome. Here are a few ways to deal with nerves:

Get ready for the meeting. The more pre-arranged you are for the meeting, the less apprehensive you will feel. Make certain to work on addressing normal inquiries and to investigate the organization and the job.

Take full breaths. Assuming that you begin to feel anxious, take a few full breaths to quiet yourself down. Center around your breathing and attempt to unwind.

Envision achievement. Imagine yourself giving a fruitful meeting and landing the position. This will assist you with feeling more sure and ready.

By following these tips, you can deal with normal meeting difficulties and increment your odds of coming out on top.

Addressing gaps in employment or changes in career direction

Addressing gaps in employment or changes in career direction in an interview can be challenging, but it is important to be honest and transparent with the interviewer. Here are a few hints:

Be ready to examine the justification for the hole or coarse adjustment. Ponder how you will make sense of the circumstance in a positive and expert manner.

Center around your adaptable abilities and experience. Regardless of whether your business hole or profession change was not straightforwardly connected with the job you are talking about, you probably have adaptable abilities and experience that are significant. Feature these abilities and involvement with your meeting.

Make sense of how you have utilized your time during the hole. On the off chance that you were jobless, make sense of how you invested your energy beneficially, for example, chipping in, taking courses, or dealing with independent ventures.

Be positive and excited. Show the questioner that you are amped up for the open door and that you are positive about your capacity to prevail in the job.

Here is an example of how to address a gap in employment in an interview:

Interviewer: I see that you have a hole in your business history somewhere in the range of 2020 and 2022. Could you at any point educate me concerning that?

Candidate: Indeed, I was jobless for that timeframe. During that time, I chose to set aside some margin to head out and to zero in on my self-awareness. I likewise took a few web-based courses to master new abilities. I'm presently anxious to get back to the labor force and I'm sure that I can make a huge commitment to your organization.

This answer is compelling on the grounds that it:

Tell the truth and be straightforward.

Centers around adaptable abilities and experience.

Makes sense of how the up-and-comer utilized their time during the hole.

Is positive and excited.

It is likewise essential to take note that you don't need to unveil each of the subtleties of your business hole or profession change. Assuming you are open to examining what is going on in more detail, you can do as such. In any case, in the event that you are not happy talking about the circumstance exhaustively, you are not committed to do as such.

Keep in mind, the questioner is attempting to become familiar with your abilities and experience to decide whether you are ideal for the job. Tell the truth and straightforwardly, and center around how you can add to the organization.

Dealing with stress, anxiety, and unexpected curveball questions

Dealing with stress, anxiety, and unexpected curveball questions is a common challenge in interviews. Here are some tips to help you through these situations:

Stress and anxiety

Before the interview:

Prepare as much as possible. The more pre-arranged you are, the less focused on you will feel. Work on responding to normal inquiries and exploring the organization and the job.

Get a good night's sleep. Being well-rested will help you to think clearly and perform your best.

Eat a healthy breakfast. Stay away from sweet food varieties and beverages, which can cause you to feel unsteady. Instead, opt for a complex carbohydrate and protein-rich breakfast, such as oatmeal with berries and nuts.

Arrive early. This will give you an opportunity to unwind and gather your contemplations before the meeting starts.

During the interview:

Take deep breaths. If you start to feel stressed or anxious, take some deep breaths to calm yourself down.

Focus on the present moment. Try not to stress over what occurred before or what could occur from here on out. Focus on the present moment and on answering the question that the interviewer is asking.

If you need a moment, ask for it. It's perfectly okay to ask the interviewer for a moment to collect your thoughts before answering a question.

Curveball questions

Before the interview:

Practice answering unexpected questions. There are a number of resources available online and in books that can help you practice answering unexpected questions.

Be prepared to think on your feet. Curveball questions are designed to assess your critical thinking skills and your ability to think on your feet.

During the interview:

Don't panic. It's normal to feel a little flustered when you're asked a curveball question. Take a full breath and give yourself a second to think.

Ask for clarification if needed. On the off chance that you don't figure out the inquiry, request that the questioner explain it.

Be honest and authentic. Don't try to make up an answer that you think the interviewer wants to hear. Tell the truth and be legitimate in your reaction.

In the event that you don't have the foggiest idea about the response, it's alright to say as much. It's better to say that you don't know the answer than to give a wrong answer.

Here is an example of how to answer a curveball question:

Interviewer: If you could be any animal, what animal would you be and why?

Candidate: I would be a dog because dogs are loyal, friendly, and always happy to see their owners. They also have a strong work ethic and are always willing to learn new things.

This answer is effective because it:

Is creative and unexpected.

Highlights the candidate's positive qualities.

Relates to the candidate's career goals.

Remember, the interviewer is trying to learn more about your skills, experience, and personality. Be honest, authentic, and confident.

CHAPTER 9:
Post-Interview Strategies

After completing a job interview, your efforts don't stop. Post-interview strategies are crucial for leaving a lasting impression and increasing your chances of securing the position. Here's a guide on effective post-interview strategies:

**1. Send a Thank-You Email:

Timely and Grateful:

Send a customized thank-you email in no less than 24 hours of the meeting.

Express gratitude for the opportunity, reiterate your interest in the position, and mention a specific aspect of the interview that resonated with you.

Here is an example of a post-interview thank-you note:

Dear [Interviewer Name],

I am writing to thank you for taking the time to interview me for the [Position Name] position yesterday. I enjoyed learning more about the role and the [Company Name] team.

I was particularly interested in our discussion about [Specific topic discussed in the interview]. I am confident that my skills and experience in [Relevant skill or experience] would be a valuable asset to your team.

Thank you again for your time and thought. I anticipate hearing from you soon.

Sincerely,

[Your Name]

**2. Reiterate Your Interest:

Affirm Your Enthusiasm:

Reiterate your interest in the role and the company in your thank-you email.

Mention why you are excited about the opportunity and how your skills align with the position.

**3. Highlight Your Fit:

Connect the Dots:

Use the thank-you email to reinforce how your skills and experiences align with the company's needs.

Underscore how you can add to the association's prosperity.

**4. Clarify Unaddressed Points:

Cover Any Missed Information:

If there were any points you didn't get a chance to discuss during the interview, address them in your thank-you email.

This can be an opportunity to add information that strengthens your candidacy.

**5. Express Confidence:

Project Confidence:

Convey confidence in your thank-you email.

Emphasize that you are eager to contribute and confident in your ability to excel in the role.

**6. Follow Up on Timelines:

Understand the Next Steps:

If the interviewer provided a timeline for the hiring process, follow up accordingly.

Politely inquire about the next steps if the timeline has passed.

**7. Send Additional Materials:

Relevant Portfolio Items:

If applicable, send additional materials that support your candidacy.

This could include a portfolio, samples of your work, or any other relevant documents.

**8. Connect on LinkedIn:

Professional Networking:

Connect with your interviewers on LinkedIn.

Craft a personalized connection message expressing your gratitude for the interview and your enthusiasm about the potential collaboration.

**9. Maintain Professionalism:

Consistent Communication:

If you need to follow up, maintain professionalism in your communication.

Be concise, polite, and express your continued interest.

**10. Reflect on the Interview:

- Self-Evaluation:

- Reflect on the interview process.

- Consider what went well, areas for improvement, and any additional points you'd like to address in future conversations.

**11. Prepare for Additional Rounds:

- Continuous Preparation:

- If there are additional interview rounds, continue your preparation.

- Anticipate potential questions and refine your responses based on your reflections from the initial interview.

**12. Stay Engaged with the Company:

- Show Ongoing Interest:

- Stay engaged with the company by following them on social media and staying informed about industry news.

- This shows your ongoing interest in the organization.

**13. Respond Promptly to Follow-Up Requests:

- Timely Responses:

- If the company requests additional information or follow-up actions, respond promptly.

- This demonstrates your efficiency and commitment.

**14. Manage Multiple Offers (if applicable):

- Communicate Clearly:

- If you receive multiple job offers, communicate transparently with each company.

- Express appreciation for the offers and request any necessary time to make a decision.

**15. Continue Job Search (if applicable):

- Keep Exploring Opportunities:

- While awaiting a response, continue exploring other job opportunities.

- This ensures you have alternative options and can make informed decisions.

**16. Prepare for Negotiations:

- Know Your Worth:

- If you receive a job offer, be prepared for negotiations.

- Research industry standards for compensation and benefits to ensure a fair package.

**17. Gracefully Accept or Decline Offers:

- Tactful Communication:

- If you receive a job offer, respond with gratitude and tact.
- If declining, express appreciation for the offer and provide a brief, professional explanation.
**18. Seek Feedback (if not successful):
- Constructive Input:
- If you're not selected for the position, consider politely requesting feedback.
- Utilize this contribution to improve your presentation in ongoing meetings.
Keep in mind, your post-interview activities add to the general effect you have with the organization. Showing appreciation, excitement, and incredible skill makes way for a positive relationship, whether you land the work or keep investigating different open doors.

Follow-up etiquette and best practices

Follow-up decency and best practices are critical for keeping a specialist picture and growing your chances of beating the competition in new worker screenings and other master settings. Here are a few hints:

Timing

Send a card to say thanks in something like 24 hours of the meeting. On the off chance that you are circling back to an employment form, send a subsequent email or shout toward one to about fourteen days, contingent upon the recruiting course of events.

Personalization

Address your subsequent message to the particular individual you talked with or who is taking care of your application. Customize your message by referencing something explicit from the meeting or application process.

Curtness

Keep your subsequent message brief and forthright. Offer your gratitude for the examiner's time and underscore your benefit in the position.

Impressive skill

Edit your subsequent message cautiously to guarantee that it is liberated from blunders. Use a specialist tone and do whatever it takes not to use work related conversation or relaxed language.

Constancy

In the event that you don't get a reaction to your underlying development, you might send a second subsequent following possibly 14 days.

Be that as it may, don't be excessively pushy. In the event that you don't get a reaction to your second development, it is ideal to continue on.

Here are a few extra ways to follow up successfully:

Be explicit about the thing you are circling back to. For instance, in the event that you are circling back to a new employee screening, notice the particular position you talked with for and the date of the meeting.

Express your motivation plainly and compactly. For instance, assuming you are following up to expressly thank the questioner for their time, say as much.

Be deferential to the questioner's time. Keep your message brief and forthright.

Edit your message cautiously prior to sending it.

Be steady, yet all the equivalent not pushy. In case you don't get a response to your fundamental turn of events, you could send a second result following perhaps 14 days. Nevertheless, if you don't get a response to your subsequent turn of events, it is ideal to progress forward.

By following these tips, you can show your shocking skill and energy, and expand your possibilities, overwhelming the opposition as you continue looking for business and other expert undertakings.

Evaluating and learning from interview experiences for continuous improvement

Assessing and gaining from your meeting encounters can assist you with constantly further developing your talking abilities and increment your odds of coming out on top in later meetings. Here are a few hints:

Following the meeting

Requires a couple of moments to consider how the meeting went. What worked out positively? What might you at some point move along?

Record your considerations and encounters while they are still new in your psyche.

Recognize any key regions where you figure you could further develop your talking abilities.

A couple of days after the meeting

Survey your notes and reflections from the meeting.

Search for designs in your criticism. Are there particular regions where you are reliably battling?

Whenever you have distinguished a few regions for development, foster an arrangement to address them. For instance, on the off chance that you are battling to respond to conduct questions, work on responding to normal social inquiries with a companion or partner.

After some time

Monitor your headway and make acclimations to your arrangement depending on the situation.

Keep on rehearsing your meeting abilities and consider your encounters.

Request input from companions, family, and associates.

Here are a particular things to assess in your meeting encounters:

Your readiness: How very much did you plan for the meeting? Did you investigate the organization and the position? Did you work on addressing normal inquiries?

Your show: How could you introduce yourself during the meeting? Might it be said that you were certain and proficient? Did you visually connect and talk plainly?

Your solutions to questions: Were your responses clear, brief, and instructive? Did you utilize explicit guides to help your focus? Did you try not to meander aimlessly or going off on digressions?

Your inquiries for the questioner: Did you pose insightful inquiries about the organization and the position? Did you try not to pose inquiries that could be handily replied by perusing the expected set of responsibilities or site?

Your development: Did you send a card to say thanks in something like 24 hours of the meeting? Did you follow up in the event that you didn't hear back from the questioner?

By assessing your meeting encounters and gaining from your mix-ups, you can constantly further develop your talking abilities and increment your odds of coming out on top in later meetings.

CONCLUSION

As we wrap up this excursion together, we should pause for a minute to ponder the procedures and experiences we've investigated. Consider this a tool stash — loaded up with useful hints, individual marking methodologies, and a nonstop improvement outlook — that you can convey into each step of your pursuit of employment.

Recap of Our Excursion:

We've covered a ton, from excelling at meetings to building a convincing individual brand. Every part was a piece of the riddle, expecting to outfit you with the information and certainty expected to explore the serious work market.

Consistent Improvement: The Mystery ingredient:

All through our conversations, the idea of nonstop improvement has been a steady friend. It's not only an extravagant term; a mentality urges you to gain from each insight, adjust your methodologies, and become both by and by and expertly. Embrace it, and you'll find that difficulties become venturing stones, and difficulties become open doors.

Applying Your Insight:
Presently, outfitted with this tool compartment, now is the right time to set the information in motion. Tailor your resume, recount your story with certainty utilizing the STAR technique, and move toward interviews realizing that you've arranged completely. This isn't about flawlessness; it's tied in with displaying your best self.

Move toward Meetings Like an Ace:
Envision strolling into a meeting room or signing into a virtual gathering with the confirmation that you have this. The readiness, the individual brand you've created, and the

flexibility you've developed — they're all helping you out. Move toward interviews not as tests, but rather as discussions where you get to sparkle and share your remarkable assets.

An Excursion, Not an Objective:

Your profession is an excursion, and this is only one section. The techniques we've examined aren't only for finding some work; they're deep rooted allies for a fruitful profession. Apply them when you're work hunting, yet as devices for constant development and achievement.

Wishing You Achievement:

As you make the following strides in your vocation process, recollect that achievement isn't an objective; it's a progression of purposeful, professional advances. Praise your triumphs, gain from your encounters, and continue to refine your methodology. You have the right stuff, the attitude, and the strength — presently go out there and do something significant.

May your process be loaded up with energizing open doors, significant associations, and the acknowledgment of your expert dreams. Good luck — you have this!